W9-AEP-079

QUICK
ONLINE JOB SEARCH

Seven Steps to Using the Internet to Find a Job

Michael Farr
and
The Editors @ JIST

Contents

JIST Works
America's Career Publisher

Quick Online Job Search

© 2011 by JIST Publishing

Published by JIST Works, an imprint of JIST Publishing
7321 Shadeland Station, Suite 200
Indianapolis, IN 46256-3923
Phone: 800-648-JIST   Fax: 877-454-7839   E-mail: info@jist.com

Visit our Web site at **www.jist.com** for information on JIST, free job search tips, tables of contents, sample pages, and ordering instructions for our many products!

Quantity discounts are available for JIST books. Please call our Sales Department at 800-648-5478 for a free catalog and more information.

Contributing Authors: Lori Cates Hand; Dave Anderson; Laurence Shatkin, Ph.D.
Cover and Interior Designer: Aleata Halbig
Proofreader: Jeanne Clark

Printed in the United States of America
15 14 13 12 11 10   9 8 7 6 5 4 3 2 1

Package of 10
ISBN 978-1-59357-855-8

The Seven Steps for a Quick Online Job Search

The process of finding a job is evolving quickly as technology gives us faster and easier ways of going about it. But even with all the recent changes, the best way to get a job is still to go out and get interviews. And the best way to get interviews is to make a job out of getting a job.

We've taken the basic truths of job hunting success and updated them for the Internet age. This book shows you how to use the Internet most effectively in all phases of your search.

1. Define Your Ideal Job
2. Identify Your Skills Online
3. Use Online Social Networking Sites to Network for Jobs
4. Find Job Openings Online
5. Organize Your Job Search
6. Use Your Resume Online
7. Correspond with Employers over E-mail

So, without further delay, let's get started!

STEP 1: Define Your Ideal Job

Too many people look for a job without clearly knowing what they are looking for. Before you go out seeking a job, we suggest that you first define exactly what you want—not just *a job* but *the job*.

Most people think that a job objective is the same as a job title, but it isn't. You need to consider other elements of what makes a job satisfying for you. Then, later, you can decide what that job is called and what industry it might be in. You can compromise on what you consider your ideal job later if you need to.

Factors to Consider

Many things go into deciding which job fits best. You need to consider your education and knowledge, the type of people you want to work with, what environment you want to work in, what city or geographic area you want to work in, how much money you need to make, how much responsibility you will accept, and what your other personal values are. Once you have your job choices narrowed down, you also need to consider your skills (see step 2).

SEVEN FACTORS TO CONSIDER IN DEFINING YOUR IDEAL JOB

As you try to define your ideal job, consider the following important questions. When you know what you want, your task then becomes finding a position that is as close to your ideal job as possible.

1. **What type of special knowledge do you have?** Perhaps you know how to fix computers, keep accounting records, or cook food. Write down the things you know from schooling, training, hobbies, family experiences, and other sources. One or more of these knowledge areas could make you a very desirable applicant in the right setting.

   _____

   _____

2. **With what types of people do you prefer to work?** Do you like to work with competitive people, or do you prefer hardworking people, creative personalities, relaxed people, or some other types?

   _____

   _____

3. **What type of work environment do you prefer?** Do you want to work inside, outside, in a quiet place, in a busy place, or in a clean or messy place; or do you want to have a window with a nice view? List the types of environments you prefer.

   _____

   _____

4. **Where do you want your next job to be located—in what city or region?** If you are open to living and working anywhere, what would your ideal community be like? Near a bus line? Close to a childcare center? Urban or rural?

   _____

   _____

5. **What benefits or income do you hope to have in your next job?** Many people will take less money or fewer benefits if they like a job in other ways—or if they need a job quickly to survive. Think about the minimum you would take as well as what you would eventually like to earn. Your next job will probably pay somewhere in between.

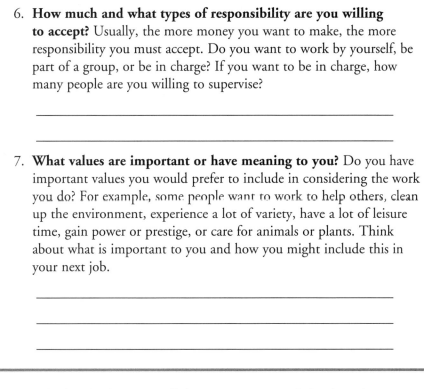

_____

_____

6. **How much and what types of responsibility are you willing to accept?** Usually, the more money you want to make, the more responsibility you must accept. Do you want to work by yourself, be part of a group, or be in charge? If you want to be in charge, how many people are you willing to supervise?

_____

_____

7. **What values are important or have meaning to you?** Do you have important values you would prefer to include in considering the work you do? For example, some people want to work to help others, clean up the environment, experience a lot of variety, have a lot of leisure time, gain power or prestige, or care for animals or plants. Think about what is important to you and how you might include this in your next job.

_____

_____

_____

Can you find a job that meets all the criteria you just defined? Perhaps. Some people do. The harder you look, the more likely you are to find it. But you will likely need to compromise, so it is useful to know what is *most* important to include in your next job. Go back over your responses to the seven factors and mark a few of those that you would most like to have or include in your ideal job.

FACTORS I WANT IN MY IDEAL JOB

Write a brief description of your ideal job. Don't worry about a job title, whether you have the necessary experience, or other practical matters yet.

_____

_____

_____

How Can You Explore Specific Job Titles and Industries?

You might find your ideal job in an occupation you haven't considered yet. And, even if you are sure of the occupation you want, it may be in an industry that is unfamiliar to you. This combination of occupation and industry forms the basis for your job search, and you should consider a variety of options.

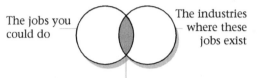

The jobs you could do — The industries where these jobs exist

Your ideal job exists in the overlap of those jobs that interest you most *and* in those industries that best meet your needs and interests!

There are thousands of job titles. Many jobs are highly specialized and employ just a few people. Although one of these more specialized jobs might be just what you want, most work falls within more general job titles that employ large numbers of people.

Use the Occupational Outlook Handbook *to Learn About Jobs*

The U.S. Department of Labor's Bureau of Labor Statistics has done extensive research on careers in the workforce. They publish a biannual guide to nearly 300 of the top jobs in the U.S. workforce, called the *Occupational Outlook Handbook (OOH)*. It tells the nature of the work, training and other qualifications needed, number of people in the job, future outlook for job openings, earnings, related occupations, and additional information and links.

OOH data is available online at www.bls.gov/oco/.

Use one of these two ways to find jobs that interest you in the *OOH:*

- Browse job titles by type (managerial, professional, service, and so on) by clicking one of the 11 links on the left side of the page.

- Browse all of the occupations alphabetically by going to the index (www.bls.gov/oco/ooh_index.htm).

Make a list of the 10 job titles that sound most interesting to you.

MY TOP 10 MOST INTERESTING JOB TITLES	
1.	_____
2.	_____
3.	_____
4.	_____
5.	_____
6.	_____
7.	_____
8.	_____
9.	_____
10.	_____

Consider Major Industries

What industry you work in is often as important as the career field. For example, some industries pay much better than others, some are growing faster than others, and others may simply be more interesting to you.

The Labor Department's *Career Guide to Industries* contains very helpful reviews for each of the major industries mentioned in the following list. You can read more about these industries at www.bls.gov/oco/cg/.

- **Natural resources, construction, and utilities:** Agriculture, forestry, and fishing; construction; mining; utilities.

- **Manufacturing:** Aerospace product and parts manufacturing; chemical manufacturing, except drugs; computer and electronic product manufacturing; food manufacturing; machinery manufacturing; motor vehicle and parts manufacturing; pharmaceutical and medicine manufacturing; printing; steel manufacturing; textile, textile product, and apparel manufacturing.

- **Trade:** Automobile dealers; clothing, accessory, and general merchandise stores; grocery stores; wholesale trade.

- **Transportation:** Air transportation; truck transportation and warehousing.

- **Information:** Broadcasting; motion picture and video industries; publishing, except software; software publishing; telecommunications.

- **Financial activities:** Banking; insurance; securities, commodities, and other investments.

- **Professional and business services:** Advertising and public relations services; computer systems design and related services; employment services; management, scientific, and technical consulting services; scientific research and development services.

- **Education, health care, and social services:** Child daycare services; educational services; health care; social assistance, except child daycare.

- **Leisure and Hospitality:** Arts, entertainment, and recreation; food services and drinking places; hotels and other accommodations.

- **Government and advocacy, grantmaking, and civic organizations:** Advocacy, grantmaking, and civic organizations; federal government; state and local government, except education and health care.

THE INDUSTRIES THAT INTEREST YOU MOST

Select the industries that interest you most and list them below.

1. _____

2. _____

3. _____

4. _____

5. _____

The jobs and industries that you identified in this step are the ones you should research most carefully. Your ideal job is likely to be found in some combination of these jobs and industries, or in more specialized but related jobs and industries.

One survey of employers found that about 90 percent of the people they interviewed might have the required job skills, but they could not describe those skills and thereby prove that they could do the job they sought. They could not answer the basic question "Why should I hire you?"

Now that you've narrowed down a list of careers that interest you, it's helpful to know what skills are needed to do those jobs. Knowing and describing your skills is essential to doing well in interviews. But if you find you don't have (and can't acquire) the needed skills, you might decide to investigate other careers instead.

We'll show you online and offline ways of identifying skills needed for your top job choices. But first, you need to know about the various types of skills.

The Three Types of Skills

Most people think of their skills as job-related skills, such as using a computer. But we all have other types of skills that are important for success on a job—and that are important to employers. The triangle that follows arranges skills in three groups, and this is a very useful way to think about skills as you use this book.

Let's look at these three types of skills—self-management, transferable, and job-related.

> ### Quip
> We all have thousands of skills. Consider the many skills required to do even a simple thing like ride a bike or bake a cake. But, of all the skills you have, employers want to know those key skills you have that enable you to do the job they need done. You must clearly identify these key skills and then emphasize them in interviews and on your resume.

Self-Management Skills

Self-management skills (also known as *adaptive skills* or *personality traits*) are the things that make you a good worker. They describe your basic personality and your ability to adapt to new environments, as well as provide the foundation for other skills. They are some of the most important skills to emphasize in interviews, yet most job seekers don't realize their importance—and don't mention them.

Some examples of these types of skills are honesty, punctuality, productivity, and creativity.

It's not bragging if it's true. Using your new skills language may be uncomfortable at first, but employers need to learn about your skills. So practice saying positive things about the skills you have for the job. If you don't, who will?

Transferable Skills

Transferable skills are skills that can be used on more than one job. Often these skills are things that you naturally do well or that are an essential part of your personality; they often are the foundations for other skills. We all have skills that can transfer from one job or career to another. For example, the ability to organize events could be used in a variety of jobs and may be essential for success in certain occupations.

Job-Related Skills

Job content or *job-related skills* are those you need to do a particular occupation. A carpenter, for example, needs to know how to use various tools. Often you can learn job-related skills on the job.

Identifying the Skills You Need

Now that you know what skills are, think about your ideal job (or jobs) that you identified in step 1. The following sections will help you identify the skills needed to do that job. If these are skills you have or can learn, that's great. You'll want to emphasize them (with examples) in interviews and on your resume. If you know that you don't have these skills, you might consider looking up the needed skills for your other choices and see whether these are more appealing to you.

Identifying Self-Management Skills

Self-management or adaptive skills are so basic to our personalities that they show up in everything we do. Even if you have never held a job, you can probably recognize self-management skills that you used in school or in leisure-time activities. All you really need is a thorough checklist that lets you think about the full range of self-management skills and check off those that characterize you. You'll find one such checklist at www. wisconsinjobcenter.org/publications. Next to Self-management Skills, click either PDF or HTML.

Formal job postings often state the self-management skills needed to perform the job well. But because these often are not spelled out, it's helpful to know the kinds of adaptive skills that most employers seek.

Self-Management Skills That Employers Value Most

According to Quintessential Careers (www.quintcareers.com), employers value the following self-management skills most:

1. Honesty/integrity/morality
2. Adaptability/flexibility
3. Tenacity/dedication/hardworking/work ethic
4. Dependability/reliability/responsibility
5. Loyalty
6. Energy/positive attitude/motivation/passion
7. Professionalism
8. Self-confidence
9. Self-motivated/ability to work with little or no supervision
10. Willingness to learn

Identifying Transferable Skills

Transferable skills are skills that you can take with you from one job to another. They're more tangible and concrete than self-management skills, but they aren't as specific as job-related skills.

A good place to discover the important skills for your top jobs is at O*NET Online (http://online. onetcenter.org).

Follow these steps from the main page:

1. Type each name of the careers that interest you in the Occupation Search box.

2. Choose from the list of results and click the job link that's closest to what you're looking for.

3. Click the Skills link and you'll see a list of the most important transferable skills for that job.

Quip

For any self-management skills that you choose to mention in interviews and on your resume, be sure to have an example of a time when you used that skill successfully. The Job Center of Wisconsin checklist exercise mentioned previously encourages you to do this.

In the following worksheet, write your target job title on the top line. Then write the list of transferable skills for that job. Make additional copies of this worksheet for the other jobs that interest you.

TRANSFERABLE SKILLS REQUIREMENT WORKSHEET

My Top Job: _____

Top Skills Needed:

1. _____

2. _____

3. _____

4. _____

5. _____

6. _____

7. _____

8. _____

9. _____

10. _____

TRANSFERABLE SKILLS THAT EMPLOYERS VALUE MOST

Quintessential Careers (www.quintcareers.com) compiled a list of the top transferable skills in general:

1. Communications skills (listening, verbal, written)

2. Analytical/research skills

3. Computer/technical literacy

4. Flexibility/adaptability/managing multiple priorities

5. Interpersonal abilities

6. Leadership/management skills

7. Multicultural sensitivity/awareness

8. Planning/organizing

9. Problem-solving/reasoning/creativity

10. Teamwork

To get an idea of whether you have some of these transferable skills, you can do another search of what O*NET says about skills. Only this time, look for an occupation that's close to a job you *already* have held. Don't assume that you have all of the skills that O*NET lists just because you held the job.

On the following worksheet, jot down the transferable skills you actually *used*. For each skill, list an example of how you used it on that job. You may want to duplicate this worksheet to use it for additional jobs you have held. (If you have never held a paying job, think about which skills you saw in O*NET that you have used in school or in volunteer or leisure-time activities.)

TRANSFERABLE SKILLS SUPPLY WORKSHEET

My previous job: _____

Skills used, with an example for each:

1. _____
   _____

2. _____
   _____

3. _____
   _____

4. _____
   _____

5. _____
   _____

6. _____
   _____

(continued)

(continued)

7. _____

_____

8. _____

_____

9. _____

_____

10. _____

_____

Lastly, see how well the items on the Transferable Skills Requirement Worksheets match the items on the Transferable Skills Supply Worksheet. That will give you an idea of how well prepared you are for the top jobs that interest you. If you lack a lot of the required skills, you'll probably need additional education or training. (Maybe you're already planning to get that.)

Identifying Job-Related Skills

As you can imagine, there are thousands of job-related skills. These are the very specific skills you would use on a particular job. The job ad or posting will likely list the most important of these specific skills, or you can guess what they would be by looking at the job description or job duties.

The O*NET can help you find some of the possible job-related skills for your top jobs:

1. Go to O*NET Online (http://online.onetcenter.org).

2. Type each name of the careers that interest you in the Occupation Search box.

3. Choose from the list of results and click the job link that's closest to what you're looking for.

4. Click the Abilities and Work Activities links to get an idea of the specific skills used on this job.

Next, make a list of the activities and duties you've discovered for the job or jobs you want and translate them to job-related skills. The first item is an example.

JOB-RELATED SKILLS REQUIREMENT WORKSHEET

Activity or Duty	Job-Related Skills
Getting information	Interviewing people; doing Internet research

Now, repeat this procedure, only this time using O*NET to tell you the job-related skills for a job or jobs you've *already* held. Again, make a list of the activities and duties and translate them to job-related skills.

JOB-RELATED SKILLS SUPPLY WORKSHEET

Activity or Duty	Job-Related Skills

(continued)

(continued)

_____	_____
_____	_____
_____	_____

What's Next?

Look back over your lists of skills in this step. Compare your self-management skills from the checklist exercise to the list of self-management skills that employers value most. Compare the "requirements" worksheets for transferable and job-related skills to the "supply" worksheets.

Do you have most of the required skills? For the ones you don't have, can you learn them easily? If there are any skills that you don't have and are not interested in learning and using, you might decide that the job isn't really a good fit for you. You can move that job lower on your list until you learn more about it. You might even decide not to pursue it.

Now you're armed with an extensive list of skills of all types—skills that you *do* have. Be sure to mention these skills on your resume and in interviews. You will need to think of stories about times that you used these skills successfully. Those stories, shortened to one sentence, can be an accomplishment bullet on your resume (see step 6). Or you can use them as examples in interviews when the interviewer asks, "Tell me about a time when you…."

STEP 3: Use Online Social Networking Sites to Network for Jobs

Employer surveys have found that most employers don't advertise their job openings. They most often hire people they already know, people who find out about the jobs through word of mouth, or people who happen to be in the right place at the right time. Although luck plays a part in finding job openings, you can use the tips in this step to increase your luck.

Most job seekers don't know how ineffective some traditional job hunting techniques tend to be. For example, the following chart shows that fewer than 15 percent of all job seekers get jobs from the newspaper want ads, most of which also appear online. Other traditional techniques include using public and private employment agencies, filling out paper and electronic applications, and mailing or e-mailing unsolicited resumes.

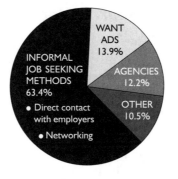

How people find jobs.

Informal, nontraditional job seeking methods have a much better success rate. These methods are active rather than passive and include making direct contact with employers and networking.

The truth is that every job search method works for someone. But experience and research show that some methods are more effective than others. Your task in the job search is to spend more of your time using more-effective methods.

Use the Two Most Effective Job Search Methods

The fact is that most jobs are not advertised, so how do you find them? The same way that about two-thirds of all job seekers do: networking with people you know (which we call making warm contacts) and directly contacting employers (which we call making cold contacts). Both of these methods are based on the job search rule you should know above all:

The Most Important Job Search Rule: Don't wait until the job opens before contacting the employer!

Employers fill most jobs with people they meet before a job is formally open. The trick is to meet people who can hire you before a job is formally available. Instead of asking whether the employer has any jobs open, we suggest that you say

> *I realize you may not have any openings now, but I would still like to talk to you about the possibility of future openings.*

Most Effective Job Search Method 1: Develop a Network of Contacts

Studies find that 40 percent of all people located their jobs through a lead provided by a friend, a relative, or an acquaintance. That makes the people you know your number-one source of job leads—more effective than all the traditional methods combined! Developing and using your contacts is called *networking,* and here's how it works:

1. **Make lists of people you know.** Make a thorough list of your friends and relatives. This list will often add up to 25 to 100 people or more. Next, think of other groups of people that you have something in common with, such as former coworkers or classmates, members of your social or sports groups, members of your professional association, former employers, neighbors, and other groups. Later in this section, you will see worksheets for doing this.

2. **Find your networking contacts on online social networking sites.** Search for former employers and coworkers, clients, and professional association members on LinkedIn (www.linkedin.com) and invite them to connect with you on the site. Search for friends and family on Facebook (www.facebook.com) and extend invitations to connect with them.

3. **Present yourself well.** Begin with your friends and relatives. Contact them via private message or over the phone. Let them know you are looking for a job and need their help. Be as clear as possible about the type of employment you want and the skills and qualifications you have. Look at the sample private message later in this step for ideas.

4. **Ask your contacts for leads.** It is possible that your contacts will know of a job opening that interests you. If so, get the details and get right on it! More likely, however, they will not, so you should ask each person the Three Magic Networking Questions.

The Three Magic Networking Questions

- **Do you know of any openings for a person with my skills?**
  If the answer is "No" (which it usually is), then ask
- **Do you know of someone else who might know of such an opening?**
  If your contact does, get that name and ask for another one. If he or she doesn't, ask
- **Do you know of anyone who might know of someone else who might know of a job opening?**
  Another good way to ask this is "Do you know someone who knows lots of people?" If all else fails, this will usually get you a name.

5. **Contact these referrals and ask them the same questions.** From each person you contact, try to get two names of other people you might contact and then e-mail, call, or invite them to connect on LinkedIn. Doing this consistently can extend your network of acquaintances by hundreds of people. Eventually, one of these people will hire you or refer you to someone who will.

If you are persistent in following these five steps, networking might be the only job search method you need. It works.

Most Effective Job Search Method 2: Contact Employers Directly

It takes more courage, but making direct contact with employers is a very effective job search technique. We call these "cold contacts" because people you don't know in advance will need to warm up to your inquiries. Two basic techniques for making cold contacts follow.

Find Potential Employers

Begin by going to an online business directory such as the Yellow Pages (www.yellow.com). Enter the kind of business you are interested in working for as well as the location in which you want to work. Look at the list of results. Copy and paste the names and contact information for the companies that interest you into a spreadsheet or contact-management program (or you can just print them).

Another way to identify potential employers is through America's Career Info-Net's Employer Locator (www.acinet.org/employerlocator/). You can search for employer names by industry, job title, or location.

Once you have your list of target companies, make contact. Call each organization listed there and ask to speak to the person who is most likely to hire or supervise you—typically the manager of the business or a department head—not the personnel or human resources manager. You can also search through each employer's Web site to find e-mail addresses for the people most likely to hire you. Then you can send them an e-mail like the following:

> Dear Ms. Jones,
>
> My name is Pam Standish. I am interested in a position in hotel management and am a particular admirer of Marriott's establishments in the Nashville area. I have four years of experience in sales, catering, and accounting with a 300-room hotel. I also have an associate degree in hotel management plus one year of experience with the Brady Culinary Institute.

(continued)

(continued)

During my employment, I helped double revenues from meetings and conferences and increased bar revenues by 46 percent. I have good problem-solving skills and am good with people. I am also well organized, hardworking, and detail-oriented.

I realize that you may not have an opening at this time; however, I would appreciate the opportunity to meet with you for 30 minutes to discuss your hotels and future opportunities within them. When would be a good day and time for you?

Sincerely,

Pam Standish

Drop In Without an Appointment

Another effective cold contact method is to just walk into a business or organization that interests you and ask to speak to the person in charge. Although dropping in is particularly effective in small businesses, it also works surprisingly well in larger ones. Remember to ask for an interview even if there are no openings now. If your timing is inconvenient, ask for a better time to come back for an interview.

Most Jobs Are with Small Employers

Businesses and organizations with fewer than 250 employees employ half of all workers and create more than 75 percent of all new jobs each year. They are simply too important to overlook in your job search! Many of them don't have personnel departments, which makes direct contacts even easier and more effective.

Find Your Network Online

You might think that you don't have a very big network. But when you start thinking of all the people you have met throughout school and your career, you will be surprised how many contacts you really have. Online social networking sites such as Facebook and business networking sites such as LinkedIn help you find all those people, get caught up, and start sharing what you're looking for (and helping others as well).

LinkedIn

Joining LinkedIn (www.linkedin.com) is an absolute must when you are networking for jobs online. It's free to join and set up a profile.

After you join, fill in your jobs and education information in your profile. A quick and easy way to do this is to upload your resume. Click the "Upload your resume" link near the top of the right side of your profile page. Use the Browse button to find your resume file (in Word, HTML, PDF, or plain-text format) on your hard drive. LinkedIn then gives you a chance to edit the information it draws from your resume. Now that you have your jobs and schools listed, your former coworkers and classmates will be able to find you more easily.

Adding Connections

Now it's time to start adding connections. Think of all the people you have worked or studied with in the past. Make a list, including how you know them. This will come in handy when you make contact with them later.

POTENTIAL LINKEDIN CONNECTIONS	
Name	*How I Know This Person*

Use the search feature to find their LinkedIn profiles. On each person's profile page, click the "Add [person] to your network" link. You'll have to tell

LinkedIn how you know the person. Then you can add a personal message. You should create a personalized message instead of using the generic one that LinkedIn recommends. Remind the person how you know them and ask whether they will join your personal network. Here's an example:

> *Dear Janet,*
>
> *We worked together on the Pepsi account at Young and Larimore back in 2006. I hope you are enjoying life as an entrepreneur. I'd like to add you as a connection on LinkedIn.*
>
> *Best,*
>
> *Phil St. John*

Then click the Send Invitation button.

After your contact has accepted your invitation, you can click the Connections link on his or her profile and see a list of his or her contacts. You can browse these lists for people you also know and send them connection invitations, too.

You can also find people by searching for particular employers, affiliations, or schools. You'll get a list of people who share these things, which might jog your memory further about people to invite to connect. Also, going forward, be sure to send connection invitations to new business contacts you meet along the way.

You don't have to limit your LinkedIn connections to people you've worked with or gone to school with. You can add personal friends, clients, service providers, family—anyone who has a profile on the site. The bigger your network, the more chances you have of finding someone who knows someone who can hire you. Just remember that your interactions here should be businesslike.

Networking Through Your Connections

Once you've built your network, you can use it to find contact people who work at your target employers. You can also ask friends to introduce you to their contacts that you don't know but who work in a company or industry that interests you.

 As with any networking relationship, LinkedIn isn't all about what people can do for you. Be ready to be asked for help, too, and be willing to help others just as you hope they will help you.

For example, say that your direct connection is linked to the nursing supervisor at a hospital near your home. You can send your connection a note such as this:

> *Dear Jim:*
>
> *Hope all is well with you and your family. I am doing well but am exploring career options. I noticed that you are connected with Susan Janowitz, the nursing supervisor at Community Health Center. I was wondering whether you would introduce me to her online. If so, would you copy us both on an e-mail and let her know that I am interested in learning more about the types of employees she's looking for now and in the future? I would really appreciate it.*
>
> *Many thanks for your help, Jim!*
>
> *Karen*

Alternatively, you can click the "Get introduced through a connection" link and ask your mutual contacts to forward an introduction through LinkedIn. Or you can send a direct message to your potential connection through the InMail feature. Just pick the method that's most comfortable to you.

After the connection is made, you can ask your questions over e-mail or set up a face-to-face informational interview to talk about the person's job and the possibility for future opportunities at the company.

LinkedIn has many other features you can use to learn more about people and companies. The more time you put into it, the more you will get out of it. Take a look at *Find a Job Through Social Networking* by Diane Crompton and Ellen Sautter for more details on getting the most out of LinkedIn.

Facebook

You might wonder how Facebook can help you find a job. After all, it can be very personal and very silly. But the fact is that the people you connect with on Facebook are likely to be your real friends and family—the people who care most about you. How can contacts get any warmer than that?

Another great plus about Facebook is how it helps you find and reconnect with people you might have forgotten about—for example, your best friend from kindergarten. You can catch up with their lives and easily start a conversation with them. It can more than double or triple the circle of people with whom you interact now.

Starting a Facebook Account

To start a Facebook account, go to www.facebook.com and fill in the details in the Sign Up box.

Next, fill in your job titles and the places you've worked, as well as the names of the schools you've attended. You can then use these links to find people you know and add them as friends. Search for your family and current friends and add them, too. Facebook will also suggest people for you to add as friends.

Because it is so tempting to share personal details on Facebook, be careful about who you add to your friends list. If you don't know and trust the person, don't add him or her.

If your Facebook account is already established, consider three important steps:

1. **Use the Privacy settings to ensure that nobody outside your friends can see what you post there.** Choose Account, Privacy Settings, and select Friends Only for all information and photos. (For added privacy, select Only Me for your phone number and other sensitive details.)

2. **Separate your personal friends from professional contacts.** Create separate lists for each type of contact (Select Account, Edit Friends, and then create and edit lists). Then you can decide how much of your personal information you want to allow each group to see.

3. **Don't post things that make you look bad.** Stay positive, don't mention controversial topics, and don't waste time playing Facebook games. Even if you've set up privacy controls correctly (which is very tricky), information can still leak out. Don't let potential employers disqualify you over something they see on Facebook.

Using Facebook to Network

So let's say you have a thriving community of Facebook friends. How can you leverage that network and get job leads? First of all, make a list of your Facebook friends who work in your target industry.

FACEBOOK FRIENDS WHO WORK IN MY TARGET INDUSTRY

_____   _____   _____

_____   _____   _____

_____   _____   _____

_____   _____   _____

_____   _____   _____

_____   _____   _____

_____   _____   _____

_____   _____   _____

_____   _____   _____

_____   _____   _____

_____   _____   _____

_____   _____   _____

Next, send each of these people a personalized private message. Click the Send [friend's name] a Message link under the photo on his or her profile page. Here's an example of what you might say:

Hey Shannon!

Long time, no see! I love the pictures of your kids—can't believe how big they're getting.

I wanted to let you know that I am currently looking for job leads and information. My town lost funding and had to cut several officer positions, including mine. I am looking for another law enforcement job in the Cleveland area. Would you happen to know of anybody who might be hiring? Maybe we could get together for coffee, catch up, and share some leads?

Thanks,

Joelle

In addition to targeted requests, you might use your status updates to keep friends posted on your job search and what you're looking for. For example:

> *Got some great leads on new law enforcement jobs near Cleveland. Excited about the possibilities!*

Network with Employers on Twitter

Twitter is a social networking site on which people share information via 140-character messages called *tweets*. Again, you might think of it as just for fun or a waste of time. But there is serious networking going on via Twitter.

In order to read other people's tweets, you must join Twitter, set up a profile, and select people to "follow."

You get just 160 characters for your bio, so be sure to sum up who you are and what you can do. Here's an example of a Twitter bio, from *The Twitter Job Search Guide* by Susan Britton Whitcomb, Chandlee Bryan, and Deb Dib:

> *I deliver double-digit profit increases in a bad economy by infusing contagious energy across the region, engaging teams, and attracting evangelistic customers.*

You can get a lot out of Twitter even if you don't send out a lot of tweets yourself. What makes Twitter unique is that you can follow strangers without them having to accept any requests from you. Then you can benefit from seeing the tweets of

- **People who work for the companies you want to work for:** Research particular people on the company's Web site and then search for their names by clicking the Find People link.

- **Employers who are hiring:** See Employers Recruiting on Twitter at http://tinyurl.com/job-hunt-org-recruiting.

- **Job search experts and HR people who give tips on how to land a job:** A good place to start is http://tweepml.org/Twitter-Job-Search-Guide/.

- **Services and people who tweet links to job postings that might interest you:** See the International Directory of 400+ Job Feeds at http://tinyurl.com/400twitjobfeeds.

- **Experts in your field whose knowledge can make you better informed for job interviews:** Try clicking the Browse Interests tab on the Find People page.

You can get even more out of Twitter by establishing your own Twitter persona. You can

- Share (retweet) the best tips from professionals in your field.

- Pass along links to news stories that are important developments in your industry.

- Tweet your own helpful job-related tips.

- Show just enough of your personality (20 percent of your tweets can be personal) to help people get to know you.

- Start conversations with people who tweet things that interest you.

Twitter conversations can lead to in-person meetings with people who might be able to help you.

Of course, there's lots more to learn about using Twitter to find jobs. Check out *The Twitter Job Search Guide* for much more in-depth help.

STEP 4: Find Job Openings Online

Even though networking has been proven repeatedly to be the most effective job search method, it doesn't hurt to also monitor the jobs that are formally posted. Just be sure that you don't spend so much time looking at postings that you're not out networking for the hidden jobs.

The Internet has limitations as a job search tool. While many have used it to get job leads, it has not worked well for far more. Too many assume they can simply add their resume to resume databases and employers will line up to hire them. Just like the older approach of sending out lots of resumes, good things sometimes happen, but not often.

We recommend two points that apply to all job search methods, including using the Internet:

- It is unwise to rely on just one or two methods in conducting your job search.

- It is essential that you use an active rather than a passive approach in your job search.

Using Job Boards Effectively

A *job board* is a site, such as Monster.com, CareerBuilder.com, or Yahoo! HotJobs, where employers pay to post jobs and candidates can search through the listings—usually for free. You can search through the listings without registering. But if you have registered and uploaded a copy of your resume (see step 6 for more on this), you can apply for the jobs quickly through the job board.

General Job Boards

General job boards such as Monster, CareerBuilder, and Yahoo! HotJobs list jobs in all different fields and from all over the country. They can be a good place to start if you're interested in several different fields or general entry-level jobs.

These sites have become more complex in recent years, adding features such as saved searches, job search history lists, and the ability to add job postings from other sites to your list.

To get the most out of general boards, follow these steps:

1. Register with the site as a member.

2. Upload your resume (see step 6 later in this book).

3. Search for jobs that fit your criteria and save these searches. When new jobs come up that fit these criteria, the job board will send you an e-mail or text message. This saves you from having to search the site every day.

4. Apply for interesting jobs using your uploaded resume.

WEDDLE's User's Choice Awards: Best Job Boards

WEDDLE's (www.weddles.com) is a research, publishing, consulting, and training firm dedicated to helping organizations and people maximize their success in recruiting, retention, job search, and career self-management. Each year they give User's Choice Awards to the top job boards—both general and niche. Here's who made the list in 2010:

- Absolutely Health Care
- AfterCollege.com
- AllHealthcareJobs.com
- AllRetailJobs.com
- CareerBuilder.com
- CollegeGrad.com
- CollegeRecruiter.com
- Dice.com
- DirectEmployers.com
- DiversityJobs.com
- EmploymentGuide.com
- ExecuNet
- GetTheJob.com
- Hcareers
- HealthCareerWeb.com

- HEALTHeCAREERS Network
- Indeed.com
- Job.com
- JobFox.com
- Jobing
- JobsinLogistics.com
- Monster.com
- Net-Temps.com
- SimplyHired.com
- 6FigureJobs.com
- SnagAJob.com
- TheLadders.com
- TopUSAJobs.com
- VetJobs.com
- Yahoo! HotJobs

GENERAL JOB BOARDS WORKSHEET

Decide which five general job boards you like best and will use in your search.

1. _____

2. _____

3. _____

4. _____

5. _____

Niche Boards

If you have a very good idea of what type of job you want, you might have better luck finding relevant job postings at smaller niche sites that cater to specific types of job seekers. For example,

- You can search for health care jobs at AllHealthcareJobs.com, or law enforcement jobs at PoliceOne (www.policeone.com/police-jobs-search/).

- You can find jobs in your specific location at sites such as JustCaliforniaJobs.com.

- You can find jobs for people with your level of experience at sites such as CollegeRecruiter.com.

To find a niche board that caters to your specific needs, go to Job Board Reviews (www.jobboardreviews.com/) and search using keywords or browse the listings.

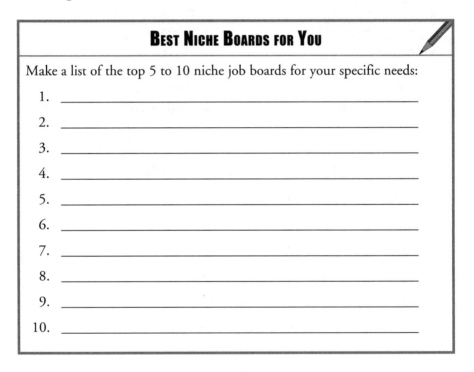

BEST NICHE BOARDS FOR YOU

Make a list of the top 5 to 10 niche job boards for your specific needs:

1. _____

2. _____

3. _____

4. _____

5. _____

6. _____

7. _____

8. _____

9. _____

10. _____

Aggregators

No search would be complete without registering at one or both of these two top job listing aggregators:

- Indeed (www.indeed.com)
- Simply Hired (www.simplyhired.com)

These sites gather up job postings from all over the Internet, including general and niche job boards, company sites, and more. Like job boards, they enable you to set up specific searches and have new jobs delivered to your e-mail and RSS feed. They also both have a feature that allows you to see job listings from the companies where your Facebook friends work (now as well as in the past).

If you have time to look at only one job listing site, make sure it's one of these two.

Company Sites

If you have a list of target companies for which you'd like to work, it only makes sense to check the careers sections of their Web sites for new postings. Often these will be posted soon after the job opening is announced. Many employers who have ceased to pay to post jobs on job boards put them on their own sites instead.

Many larger companies have tools on their careers sections that enable you to request an e-mail notification when jobs that match your criteria are posted. Some will also enable you to save your search as an RSS feed.

Other Places to Look for Job Search Openings and Help

As you know, networking is the best way to find jobs. However, here are some other options for finding openings and assistance—some of them more effective than others.

The Government Employment Service and One-Stop Centers

Each state and province has a network of local offices to pay unemployment compensation, provide job leads, and offer other services—at no charge to you or to employers. The service's name varies by region. It may be called Job Service, Department of Labor, Unemployment Office, Workforce Development, WorkOne, or another name. All of these offices are now online. You can find your local office at www.careeronestop.org.

The Employment and Training Administration Web site at www.doleta.gov gives you information on the programs provided by the government employment service, plus links to other useful sites.

Visit your local office early in your job search. Find out whether you qualify for unemployment compensation and learn more about its services. Look into it—the price is right.

Private Employment Agencies

Private employment agencies are businesses that charge a fee either to you or to the employer that hires you. Fees can be from less than one month's pay to 15 percent or more of your annual salary. You will often see these agencies' ads in the help wanted section of the newspaper. Most have Web sites.

Be careful about using fee-based employment agencies. Recent research indicates that more people use and benefit from fee-based agencies than in the past. However, relatively few people who register with private agencies get a job through them.

If you use a private employment agency, ask for interviews with the employers who agree to pay the agency's fee. Do not sign an exclusive agreement or be pressured into accepting a job. Also, continue to actively look for your own leads. You can find these agencies in the phone book's yellow pages, and many state- or province-government Web sites offer lists of the private employment agencies in their states.

Temporary Agencies

Temporary agencies offer jobs that last from several days to many months. They charge the employer an hourly fee, and then pay you a bit less and keep the difference. You pay no direct fee to the agency. Many private employment agencies now provide temporary jobs as well.

Temp agencies have grown rapidly for good reason. They provide employers with short-term help, and employers often use them to find people they might want to hire later. If the employers are dissatisfied, they can just ask the agency for different temp workers.

Temp agencies can help you survive between jobs and get experience in different work settings. Temp jobs provide a very good option while you look for long-term work, and you might get a job offer while working in a temp job. Holding a temporary job might even lead to a regular job with the same or a similar employer.

The American Staffing Association offers a way to search for temp agencies and staffing firms on its Web site: www.americanstaffing.net/jobseekers/find_company.cfm.

School and Other Employment Services

Only a small percentage of job seekers use school and other special employment services, probably because few job seekers have the service available to them. If you are a student or graduate, find out about any employment services at your school. Some schools provide free career counseling, resume writing help, referrals to job openings, career interest tests, reference materials, Web sites listing job openings, and other services. Special career programs work with veterans, people with disabilities, welfare recipients, union members, professional groups, and many others. So check out these services and consider using them.

STEP 5: Organize Your Job Search

The average job seeker gets about five interviews a month—fewer than two a week. Yet many job seekers use the methods in this book to get two interviews a day. Getting two interviews a day equals 10 a week and 40 a month. That's 800 percent more interviews than the average job seeker gets. Who do you think will get a job offer quicker?

You might think that getting two interviews a day sounds impossible. However, getting two interviews a day is quite possible if you redefine what counts as an interview and use the networking techniques from step 3.

The New Definition of an Interview: Any face-to-face contact with someone who has the authority to hire or supervise a person with your skills—even if no opening exists at the time you talk with them.

If you use this new definition, it becomes *much* easier to get interviews. You can now interview with all sorts of potential employers, not just those who have job openings now. While most other job seekers look for advertised or actual openings, you can get interviews before a job opens up or before it is advertised and widely known. You will be considered for jobs that may soon be created but that others will not know about. And, of course, you can also interview for existing openings just as everyone else does.

Spending as much time as possible on your job search and setting a job search schedule are important parts of this step. Researchers at the University of Missouri found in a 2009 study that developing and following a job search plan from the start, as well as having a positive attitude about the search, had a significant impact on job search success (*U.S. News & World Report,* September 24, 2009).

Make Your Search a Full-Time Job

Job seekers average fewer than 15 hours a week looking for work. On average, unemployment lasts three or more months, with some people out of work far longer (for example, older workers and higher earners). Years of research indicate that the more time you spend on your job search each week, the less time you will likely remain unemployed.

Of course, using the more effective job search methods presented in this book also helps. Many job search programs that teach job seekers our basic approach of using more effective methods and spending more time looking have proven that these seekers often find a job in half the average time. More importantly, many job seekers also find better jobs using these methods.

So, if you are unemployed and looking for a full-time job, you should plan to look on a full-time basis. It just makes sense to do so, although many do not, or they start out well but quickly get discouraged. Most job seekers simply don't have a structured plan—they have no idea what they are going to do next Thursday. The plan that follows will show you how to structure your job search like a job.

Decide How Much Time You Will Spend Looking for Work Each Week and Day

First and most importantly, decide how many hours you are willing to spend each week on your job search. You should spend a minimum of 25 hours a week on hardcore job search activities with no goofing around. The following worksheet walks you through a simple but effective process to set a job search schedule for each week.

PLAN YOUR JOB SEARCH WEEK

1. How many hours are you willing to spend each week looking for a job?

    _____

2. Which days of the week will you spend looking for a job?

    _____

    _____

3. How many hours will you look each day?

    _____

---

4. At what times will you begin and end your job search on each of these days?

_____

Create a Specific Daily Job Search Schedule

Having a specific daily schedule is essential because most job seekers find it hard to stay productive each day. The sample daily schedule that follows is the result of years of research into what schedule gets the best results. Mike Farr tested many schedules in job search programs he ran, and this particular schedule worked best.

A Sample Daily Schedule That Works

Time	Activity
7–8 a.m.	Get up, shower, dress, eat breakfast.
8–8:15 a.m.	Organize workspace, review schedule for today's interviews and promised follow-ups, check e-mail, and update schedule as needed.
8:15–9 a.m.	Review old leads for follow-up needed today; develop new leads from the Internet, warm contact lists, and other sources; complete daily contact list.
9–10 a.m.	Make phone calls or send e-mails to set up interviews.
10–10:15 a.m.	Take a break.
10:15–11 a.m.	Make more calls; set up more interviews.
11 a.m.–Noon	Send follow-up notes and do other office activities as needed.
Noon–1 p.m.	Break for lunch, relax.
1–3 p.m.	Go on interviews; make cold contacts in the field.
Evening	Read job search books, make calls to warm contacts not reachable during the day, work on a better resume, spend time with friends and family, exercise, relax.

Use the following worksheet to set up a daily schedule customized for your needs—and then stick to it.

A Sample Daily Schedule That Works

Time	Activity
7:00 a.m.	_____
7:30 a.m.	_____
8:00 a.m.	_____
8:30 a.m.	_____
9:00 a.m.	_____
9:30 a.m.	_____
10:00 a.m.	_____
10:30 a.m.	_____
11:00 a.m.	_____
11:30 a.m.	_____
12:00 p.m.	_____
12:30 p.m.	_____
1:00 p.m.	_____
1:30 p.m.	_____
2:00 p.m.	_____
2:30 p.m.	_____
3:00 p.m.	_____
3:30 p.m.	_____
4:00 p.m.	_____
4:30 p.m.	_____
5:00 p.m.	_____
6:00 p.m.	_____
7:00 p.m.	_____
Evening	_____

If you are not accustomed to using a daily schedule book or electronic planner, promise yourself to get a good one today. Choose one that allows for each day's plan on an hourly basis, plus daily to-do lists. Record your daily schedule in advance, and then add interviews as they come. Get used to carrying your planner with you—and use it!

Managing Your Schedule and Contacts Electronically

If you'd rather organize your job search on a computer, you can create simple forms, tables, or spreadsheets (using Microsoft Word or Excel, for example) to track the time you spend and the contacts you make. All of the worksheets in this book can be easily re-created using a word processing program.

A Web site that offers a job search planning system online is JibberJobber (www.jibberjobber.com). It's free to join the site and use its basic features. JibberJobber enables you to enter your target jobs and companies, keep track of your network, and track your interviews and networking events on its calendar.

Contact management and scheduling programs are included on most computers or can easily be found online. Programs such as Microsoft Outlook or Google Calendar (www, www.google.com/calendar) can help you keep track of your to-do lists, notify you when you have important messages, and warn you when you have appointments.

If you have a smartphone or other handheld electronic device, you can stay organized on the go. Today's smartphones come with applications for managing contacts, scheduling appointments, setting up automatic reminders, and organizing daily activities. If you have mobile Internet access, you can easily research job openings, e-mail employers, send out resumes or electronic business cards, and get a reminder that you have an interview in an hour. Be aware that most scheduling, calendar, and contact software is free or can be used as part of your e-mail, Internet, or cell phone account. It shouldn't cost much to stay organized.

Regardless of whether you use a simple sheet of paper or the latest iPhone app, as long as you always know who you are supposed to talk to, when, and where, you can keep up with your job search schedule.

DECIDE HOW YOU WILL ORGANIZE YOUR SEARCH

Check off the method(s) you will use to organize your search and add the names of specific applications and sites you plan to use.

❑ A planner book

❑ Computer applications

- _____

- _____

(continued)

(continued)

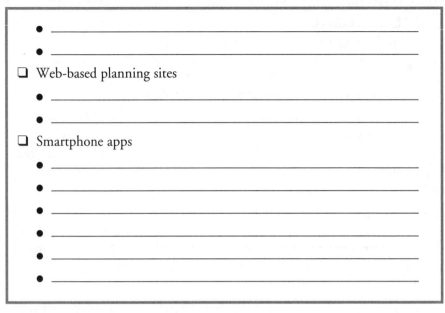

- ● _____
- ● _____
- ❑ Web-based planning sites
  - ● _____
  - ● _____
- ❑ Smartphone apps
  - ● _____
  - ● _____
  - ● _____
  - ● _____
  - ● _____
  - ● _____

STEP 6: Use Your Resume Online

Sending out resumes and waiting for responses is not an effective job seeking technique. But many employers *will* ask you for a resume, and it can be a useful tool in your job search. We suggest that you begin with a simple resume you can complete quickly. We've seen too many people spend weeks working on a resume when they could have been out getting interviews instead. If you want a better resume, you can work on it on weekends and evenings. Once you have a simple resume, you can convert it to electronic format and use it to apply for jobs online.

Write Your Resume

Most resumes use a chronological format where the most recent experience is listed first, followed by each preceding job. Most employers prefer this format. It works fine for someone with work experience in several similar jobs, but not as well for those with limited experience or for career changers. Those people might consider using a skills resume, which leads with an extensive summary of skills grouped under relevant headings. (For more on writing a skills resume, see *Quick Resume Guide* by Michael Farr and The Editors at JIST.)

Chronological Resumes

Follow these tips as you write a basic chronological resume:

- **Name:** Use your formal name (not a nickname).

- **Address and contact information:** Avoid abbreviations in your address and include your ZIP code. If you might move, use a friend's address or include a forwarding address. Most employers will not write to you, so provide reliable phone numbers, e-mail addresses, and other contact options. Always include your area code in your phone number because you never know where your resume might travel. Make sure that you have voice mail and record a professional-sounding message.

- **Job objective/professional summary statement:** You should almost always have one, even if it is general—for example "A position in the office management, accounting, or administrative assistant area that enables me to grow professionally." Simply writing "secretary" or "clerical" might limit someone from being considered for other jobs. Professional applicants might consider using an impressive summary statement instead, with a heading that states the desired job target.

- **Education and training:** Include any training or education you've had that supports your job objective. If you did not finish a formal degree or program, list what you did complete and emphasize accomplishments. If your experience is not strong, add details here such as related courses and extracurricular activities.

  New graduates should emphasize their recent training and education more than those with a few years of related work experience would. A more detailed education and training section might include specific courses you took, and activities or accomplishments that support your job objective or reinforce your key skills. Include other details that reflect how hard you work, such as working your way through school.

- **Previous experience:** Include the basics such as employer name, job title, dates employed, and responsibilities.

- **Skills and accomplishments:** Include those that support your ability to do well in the job you seek now. Even small details count. Maybe your attendance was perfect, you met a tight deadline, or you did the work of others during vacations. Be specific and include numbers—even if you have to estimate them.

- **Promotions:** If you were promoted or got good evaluations, say so: "cashier, promoted to assistant manager," for example. You can list a promotion to a more responsible job as a separate job if doing so results in a stronger resume.

- **Personal data:** Do not include irrelevant details such as height, weight, and marital status or a photo. Current laws do not allow an employer to base hiring decisions on these points. Providing this information can cause some employers to toss your resume. You can include information about hobbies or leisure activities that directly support your job objective in a special section.

- **References:** You do not need to list your references on your resume. You don't even have to say "References available upon request" on your resume. List the names and contact information of your references on a separate page and give it to employers who ask. Make sure that each reference will make nice comments about you and ask each to write a letter of recommendation that you can give to employers.

You can use the Essential Job Search Data Worksheet in the appendix (or online at www.jist.com/pdf/EJSDW.pdf) to gather information for your resume and interviews.

Skills and Combination Resumes

The alternative to a chronological resume is a skills resume. Skills resumes are most useful when there is a gap in your employment or when you are trying to change careers and want to emphasize your transferable skills over your work history. Employers do not like skills resumes in general because it's difficult to see your work history and they think you're trying to hide something. A better approach for a career changer would be to use a combination resume, which leads off with evidence of your skills but also includes a chronological list of your job history after that.

When you have a simple, errorless, and eye-pleasing resume, get on with your job search. There is no reason to delay! If you want to create a better resume, you can work on improving it in your spare time (evenings or weekends). Never delay or slow down your job search because your resume is not good enough. The best approach is to create a simple and acceptable resume as quickly as possible and then use it. As time permits, create a better one if you feel you must.

Convert Your Resume to Plain Text

Employers may ask you to send them your resume online. Pay attention to their instructions, because they will probably specify whether they want you to send your Word file as an attachment, send a PDF (created with Adobe Acrobat), or transmit a plain-text resume via e-mail or their Web site. Louise Kursmark, coauthor of *15-Minute Cover Letter,* provides these steps for converting your resume to plain text:

1. Save your resume with a different name and select "text only," "ASCII," or "Plain Text (*.txt)" in the "Save As Type" option box.

2. Reopen the file. Your word processor has automatically reformatted your resume into Courier font, removed all formatting, and left-justified the text.

3. Reset the margins to 2 inches left and right, so that you have a narrow column of text rather than a full page width. Adjust line lengths to fit within the narrow margins by adding hard returns.

4. Fix any glitches such as odd characters that may have been inserted to take the place of "curly" quotes, dashes, accents, or other nonstandard symbols.

5. Remove any tabs and adjust spacing as necessary. You might add a few extra blank spaces, move text down to the next line, or add extra blank lines for readability.

6. Consider adding horizontal dividers to break the resume into sections. You can use a row of any standard typewriter symbols, such as *, -, (,), =, +, ^, or #.

When you close the file, it will be saved with the .txt file extension. When you are ready to use it, just open the file, select and copy the text, and paste it into the online application or e-mail message. The final result should look something like the following example, from Susan Britton Whitcomb's book *Résumé Magic.*

```
SAMUEL FEINMAN
489 Smithfield Road
Salem, OR 97301
503.491.3033
samfine@earthlink.net

= = = = = = = = = = = = = = = = = = = = = =

SALES PROFESSIONAL

Dynamic, motivated, award-winning sales professional with extensive
experience. Troubleshooter and problem-solver. Team player who can
motivate self and others. Excellent management and training skills.

= = = = = = = = = = = = = = = = = = = = = =

RELATED EXPERIENCE

Jackson Chevrolet, Springfield, OR
GENERAL MANAGER, XXXX-Present
* Consistently achieve top-ten volume dealer in the Northwest.
* Manage all dealership operations including computer systems, sales,
parts, service, and administration.
* Profitably operate dealership through difficult economic times.
* Meet or exceed customer service, parts, sales, and car service
objectives.
* Maintain high-profile used-car operation.

Afford-A-Ford, Albany, OR
ASSISTANT GENERAL MANAGER, XXXX-XXXX
* Consistently in top five for sales in district; met or exceeded sales
objectives.
* Supervised and trained staff of 90.
* Helped to convert a consistently money-losing store into a profitable
operation by end of first year.
* Focused on customer satisfaction through employee satisfaction and
training.
* Built strong parts and service business, managing excellent
interaction among parts, service, and sales.
* Instituted fleet-sales department and became top fleet-sales dealer
three years running.
* Built lease portfolio from virtually none to 31% of retail.

WetWater Pool Products, Salem, OR
SALES/CUSTOMER SERVICE, XXXX-XXXX
* Advised customers to purchase products that best met their needs while
focusing attention on products more profitable to company.
* Troubleshot and solved customer problems, identifying rapid solutions
and emphasizing customer satisfaction and retention.
* Oversaw shipping and receiving staff.

= = = = = = = = = = = = = = = = = = = = = =

ADDITIONAL EXPERIENCE

State of Oregon, Salem, OR
COMPUTER TECHNICIAN INTERN, XXXX-XXXX
* Built customized computers for state offices.
* Worked with team on installation of computer systems.

= = = = = = = = = = = = = = = = = = = = = =

EDUCATION

AS, Oregon Community College, Troy, OR
Major: Business studies

= = = = = = = = = = = = = = = = = = = = = =

REFERENCES AVAILABLE ON REQUEST
```

An example of a plain-text resume that you can submit online.

Many company Web sites allow you to upload your resume file automatically. You can click the Browse button, find your resume file on your computer, and upload it. Look for instructions about which type of file the site will accept. Some will accept Word and PDF formats. For best results, though, upload your text-only resume.

Put Your Resume into Online Job Banks

Although uploading your resume to a job bank and waiting for someone to find it is a passive approach, you might as well do it. That way, if you find a job there for which you want to apply, your resume will be ready to submit with just a few clicks.

To get your resume into Monster.com's database, for example, you have three options:

- Copy and paste your resume.
- Upload your Word resume.
- Build a new resume in Monster's resume builder.

Generally the upload option is easiest. But if you don't have your resume in a format that the job board accepts, you can use the copy and paste option. If you don't have a resume at all, you can use the build option to make one.

Copy and Paste

For this option, you will want to use your text-only resume. To copy and paste your resume into Monster.com's database, follow these steps:

1. Open your text-only resume file.

2. Go to the Profile & Resume tab on Monster.com and select Resume.

3. Click the Create Resume button.

4. Select Copy & Paste from the drop-down list.

5. Fill in a name for your resume (such as your name and a date) and your target job title.

6. If you are in an active and non-confidential job search, make sure the checkbox is selected to make your resume searchable for employers. You can make only one resume active at a time, so you might decide later to change which one is active.

7. Click the Create button.

8. Go to Word, select your whole resume document (Ctrl+Shift+End), and copy it (Ctrl+C).

9. Go back to the Resume Builder window and paste your resume into it (Ctrl+V).

10. Check the resume's appearance and add spacing and line breaks if needed.

11. Click Save and Continue.

12. Click "No, thanks" to skip any "special offers."

13. Click Return to Resumes, open the new resume, and see how it looks. Make adjustments and resave if needed.

At some point, you will be asked to fill out a detailed Resume Visibility page to help make your resume easier for employers to find.

The Upload Option

If you choose to upload your Word resume, follow these steps:

1. Click the Profile & Resume tab.

2. Select the Resume option.

3. Click Create Resume.

4. Select Upload from the drop-down list.

5. Search for your resume on your hard drive using the Browse button and click to upload it.

6. Skip any "special offers" by clicking "No, thanks."

7. Click the Return to Resumes link and check the formatting of your uploaded resume. If there are problems, you can fix them and upload a new version. Bullets and fonts usually convert correctly, but it doesn't hurt to check the result.

The Build Option

This is the most time-consuming option, but you might choose it because the prompts help you put your resume in a good order.

1. Go to the Profile & Resume tab and select Resume.

2. Click the Create Resume button.

3. Select Build from the drop-down list.

4. Click the links for each section and fill in the details.

5. Add your skills and any other special sections that apply to you.

6. Click Save & Continue.

Create a Career Portfolio and Put It Online

Another way you can show prospective employers evidence of your skills and accomplishments is with a career portfolio. In fact, a portfolio provides employers with a much more complete picture of you as a worker than a resume can. The drawback is that it takes longer to put together and much longer for employers to look at.

What is a career portfolio? It is a collection of documents and artifacts placed in a binder or folder or some digital format such as a Web page or a slide show. It includes information about your work history as well as your educational background. It showcases your goals, skills, talents, values, and accomplishments. It often includes copies or records of your actual work, sometimes in the form of charts, graphs, photos, business reports, customer comments, or letters of recommendation.

Your portfolio showcases your success and reflects your career goals and values. It also demonstrates the knowledge, skills, and preferences you have that will make you an asset to the employer. In short, a portfolio tells an employer who you are and what you are capable of.

What you put in your portfolio is ultimately up to you, although it also depends on the job you are seeking. The following worksheet can help you to think about what you might include in your own portfolio.

My Portfolio Checklist
Take a moment and think about what you might put into your career portfolio. Go down the list and check off any of the materials that you would like to include.   ❏ Certifications   ❏ Complete history of paid employment

(continued)

(continued)

- ❏ Copies of evaluations
- ❏ Copies or lists of major awards
- ❏ Customer feedback forms
- ❏ Diplomas
- ❏ Evidence of volunteer efforts
- ❏ Letters of recommendation
- ❏ Licenses
- ❏ Papers, projects, or presentations given
- ❏ Personal goals or mission statement
- ❏ Records of public and community service
- ❏ Resume
- ❏ Samples of work that showcase your skills
- ❏ Transcripts
- ❏ Other_____
- ❏ Other_____
- ❏ Other_____

Paper Versus Electronic Portfolios

You can make copies of all of your materials and put them neatly in a nice, plain-colored binder to give to employers or to take with you on interviews. In fact, this is the way it used to be done. Nowadays, most career portfolios are created on the computer using common software (such as Microsoft Word or PowerPoint) or Web-based programs. Such portfolios are often called *digital portfolios* or *e-portfolios*.

A digital career portfolio contains all the information that a paper-based portfolio would, but in an electronic format. This material is then copied onto some portable media (such as a CD or flash drive) or published on a Web site.

Digital portfolios have several advantages over paper-based ones:

- You can mail your digital portfolio to an employer on a CD, send it as an e-mail attachment, or post it to your own personal Web site and direct employers to it.

- Some portfolio sites, such as carbonmade (http://carbonmade.com) and VisualCV (www.visualcv.com), allow you to create and post your portfolio for free using their programs and templates.

- Because it is all electronic, you can send your portfolio to several employers at once.

- You don't have to worry about it getting lost or destroyed.

- You can always print out a hard copy to take with you to interviews.

- You can easily import other kinds of media, such as pictures or video.

Following is a sample opening page from a digital portfolio featured in *Create Your Digital Portfolio.*

Sample digital portfolio.

If you'd like to learn more about creating a digital portfolio, visit the Web sites mentioned or see *Create Your Digital Portfolio* by Susan Amirian and Eleanor Flanigan.

Why Use a Portfolio?

In recent years, job seekers across all industries have recognized the value of portfolios. That doesn't mean that everyone has one, though. In fact, outside of a few fields such as graphic arts where they are all but required, very few job seekers take the time to create a portfolio—all the more reason why yours would stand out.

Be Very Careful What You Post

There is no denying the Internet is an incredibly powerful job search tool. But you should be careful about how much and what kind of information you put out there. Your digital self—the version of you that people get from your e-mails, postings, social networking pages, online portfolio, and personal Web site—is available to everyone, including potential employers. And they do look. According to studies, nearly half of employers check Facebook and other information found on the Internet when reviewing potential candidates. So be sure there is nothing about you online that an employer might use to screen you out.

Once you have your portfolio, the key is to get it into the hands of the person who could hire you. You shouldn't send your portfolio to every potential employer you find. In fact, we recommend contacting them first and sending them your resume. If they show an interest in you, feel free to send them your portfolio.

Alternatively, you can just use your portfolio as an interview aid. Imagine you are asked about your customer service skills or how well you get along with coworkers. Of course you can tell the interviewer your answer. But think about how much more effective it would be to show her instead, by pulling customer comment cards or letters of recommendation from coworkers from your portfolio. Think of your portfolio and the materials it contains as evidence to support your claim that you are the right person for the job.

A portfolio is not a guaranteed ticket to an interview. Most employers barely have time to look over your resume, let alone go through a 20-page record of your accomplishments. However, if you get an employer's attention, employers are usually more than happy to take a look at a portfolio—giving you the advantage.

STEP 7: Correspond with Employers over E-mail

The majority of business correspondence now happens over e-mail. The good news is that you can now make direct, instant contact with the people who can hire you. The bad news is that everyone else is doing the same thing, so hiring managers must sort through hundreds of messages every day. It's easy to get lost in the shuffle.

Another problem is that because e-mail is fast, people mistakenly think that all messages can be casual. But a cover letter that accompanies an e-mailed resume should be as formal as a printed cover letter and contain the same vital information.

In this step, you'll learn the basics of writing e-mails to employers for various purposes: To set up informational interviews, to use as cover letters when you're e-mailing a resume, and to follow up after interviews.

Setting Up Informational Interviews over E-mail

An informational interview is when you meet with someone who does not currently have a job opening but works in a company or field that interests you. The purpose of this meeting is to learn more about the job or the company and decide whether it is one you would enjoy. Also, meeting people through informational interviews is a good way to grow your network.

Here are some tips for landing and conducting successful informational interview meetings:

- Make it clear that you are not asking for a job. This way, they will not feel pressured and won't feel badly if they don't have a job available.

- Promise that you will take up only 30 minutes of the person's time— and then be sure that you respect that.

- Have a list of questions ready to ask the person about his or her job and industry.

- Bring along your resume in case the person asks to see it, but don't offer it to him unless he asks for it.

- Listen more than you talk. This meeting is all about them, not you.

You could call the person with whom you'd like to meet, but sending an e-mail might be an easier way to reach busy people who never answer their phones. In *The Career Coward's Guide to Changing Careers,* author Katy Piotrowski suggests sending an e-mail like the following:

> *Dear [Person's Name]:*
>
> *I learned of you through [resource]. I am researching more about [career field or company] as a potential career path for myself. To help with my decisions and planning, I am interviewing specialists such as yourself about your work.*
>
> *(continued)*

(continued)

Would you be willing to be interviewed about your career? The conversation would take between 15 and 30 minutes and could be conducted in person or over the phone at a time that is convenient to you.

Please let me know, and if I haven't heard from you in a day or so, I will follow up with you to make sure you received this successfully.

Many thanks,

[your name]

Quick Tips for Writing an E-mail Cover Letter in 15 Minutes

However you submit your resume, it is important to provide a letter along with your resume that explains why you are sending it—a cover letter or cover message. Even resume banks often have a place where you can upload or paste a cover letter. A cover letter highlights your key qualifications; explains your situation; and asks the recipient for some specific action, consideration, or response.

No matter to whom you are writing, virtually every good cover letter should follow these guidelines.

1. Write to Someone in Particular

Avoid sending a cover letter "To whom it may concern" or using some other impersonal opening. We all get enough junk mail, and if you don't send your letter to someone by name, it will be treated like junk mail.

2. Make Absolutely No Errors

One way to offend people right away is to misspell their names or use incorrect titles. If you are not 100 percent certain, call and verify the correct spelling of the name and other details before you send the letter. (Often you can find correct spellings and titles on the company's Web site, too.) Also, review your letters carefully to be sure that they contain no typographical, grammatical, or other errors.

3. Personalize Your Content

No one is impressed by form letters, and you should not use them. Those computer-generated letters that automatically insert a name (known as merge mailings) never fool anyone, and cover letters done in this way are offensive. Small, targeted mailings to a carefully selected group of prospective employers can be effective if you tailor your cover letter to each recipient, but large mass mailings are a waste of time. If you can't customize your letter in some way, don't send it.

4. Present a Good Appearance

Use a standard letter format that complements your resume type and format. You might find it easier to use your word-processing software's template functions than to create a format from scratch. Your letters don't have to be fancy, but they do have to look professional.

5. Begin with a Friendly Opening

Start your letter by sharing the reason you are writing and, if appropriate, a reminder of any prior contacts or the name of the person who referred you. See page 50 for an example of how to begin your letter.

6. Target Your Skills and Experiences

To effectively target your skills and experiences, you must know something about the organization, the job opportunity, or the person with whom you are dealing. Present any relevant background that may be of particular interest to the person to whom you are writing.

7. Close with an Action Statement

Don't close your letter without clearly identifying what you will do next. Don't leave it up to the employer to contact you, because that doesn't guarantee a response. Close on a positive note and let the employer know how and when you will be following up.

Dear Ms. Gold:

My sister, Tracy Oswald, tells me that you are looking for a systems administrator for your growing San Francisco operation.

I am experienced, reliable, loyal, and customer focused and would like to talk with you about joining your team.

The enclosed resume describes nearly 15 years of experience with Anthem Blue Cross/Blue Shield, during which I advanced to increasingly responsible technical positions. Whether independently or with a team, I worked hard to provide the best possible service and support to my "customers." I was recognized for my strong technical skills, ability to guide less experienced support people, and 100% reliability.

A recent downsizing at Anthem caused my position to be eliminated, and I am looking for a new opportunity with a company like yours, where my technical abilities, positive attitude, and dedication will be valued.

I will call you next week in hopes of getting together soon.

Yours truly,

Kevin Oswald

****
Attachment: resume

Sample E-mail Cover Letter (Written by Louise Kursmark)

Adapt Your JIST Card into an E-mail Signature

A key part of our job search strategy has always been the JIST Card. JIST Cards have been used by thousands of job search programs and millions of people. Employers like their direct and timesaving format, and they have been proven as an effective tool to get job leads. Attach one to your resume. Give them to friends, relatives, and other contacts and ask them to pass them along to others who might know of an opening. Enclose them in thank-you notes after interviews. Leave one with employers as a business card. However you get them in circulation, you may be surprised at how well they work.

You can easily create JIST Cards on a computer and print them on card stock you can buy at any office-supply store. Or you can have a few hundred printed cheaply by a local quick-print shop. Although they are often done as 3-by-5 cards, they can be printed in any size or format, including standard business card size.

Sandy Nolan

Position: General Office/Clerical

Cell phone: (512) 232-9213

Email: snolan@aol.com

More than two years of work experience plus one year of training in office prac-
tices. Type 55 wpm, trained in word processing, post general ledger, have good
interpersonal skills, and get along with most people. Can meet deadlines and
handle pressure well.

Willing to work any hours.

Organized, honest, reliable, and hardworking.

Richard Straightarrow

Home: (602) 253-9678
Cell: (602) 257-6643
E-mail: RSS@email.com

Objective: **Electronics installation, maintenance, and sales**

Four years of work experience plus a two-year A.S. degree in Electronics Engineering
Technology. Managed a $360K annual business while attending school full time, with
grades in the top 25%. Familiar with all major electronic diagnostic and repair equipment.
Hands-on experience with medical, consumer, communication, and industrial electronics
equipment and applications. Good problem-solving and communication skills.
Customer service oriented.

Willing to do what it takes to get the job done.

Self-motivated, dependable, learn quickly.

Sample JIST Cards

But if you're making a lot of contacts online, it doesn't hurt to put a con-
densed version of your JIST Card content at the bottom of your e-mail messages. This is called a *signature*. Here's how the second JIST Card above might
look as an e-mail signature:

Richard Straightarrow
A.S., Electronics Engineering Technology
Home: (602) 253-9678 / Cell: (602) 257-6643 / RSS@email.com
Seeking a position in electronics installation, maintenance, and sales.
* Four years of experience.
* Familiar with all major diagnostic and repair equipment.
* Customer service orientation, problem solver, self-motivated,
  dependable.

WRITE YOUR E-MAIL SIGNATURE LINE

Use this worksheet to write a short but information-packed e-mail signature line:

_____

_____

_____

_____

_____

_____

_____

_____

_____

If you are using Microsoft Outlook to send e-mail, follow these steps to set up your e-mail signature:

1. Select Tools, Options, and the Mail Format tab.

2. Click the Signatures button.

3. Type or paste your text into the text box.

4. Adjust the fonts and formatting as needed.

5. Click the two OK buttons.

Now, whenever you send anyone an e-mail, your JIST Card information will be at the bottom. This is helpful not only for when you e-mail potential employers, but also for when you contact friends. You never know who might see it and realize that they have a lead for you.

Interviewing Tips

Beyond researching company information beforehand, the Internet can't help you much when it comes to interviews. You have to do those in person. Nonetheless, this book wouldn't be complete without some interviewing advice:

- **Make a good impression before you arrive.** Your resume, e-mails, applications, and other written correspondence create an impression before the interview, so make them professional and error free.

- **Do some homework on the organization before you go.** You can often get information on a business and on industry trends from the Internet. Try researching the company at Hoovers (www.hoovers.com) and individual company Web sites.

- **Dress and groom the same way the interviewer is likely to be dressed—but better!** Employer surveys find that almost half of all people's dress or grooming creates an initial negative impression. So this is a big problem. If necessary, get advice on your interviewing outfits from someone who dresses well. Pay close attention to your grooming, too—little things do count.

- **Be early.** Leave in plenty of time to be a few minutes early to an interview.

- **Be friendly and respectful with the receptionist.** Doing otherwise will often get back to the interviewer and result in a quick rejection.

- **Follow the interviewer's lead in the first few minutes.** The interview often begins with informal small talk, but the interviewer uses this time to see how you interact. This is a good time to make a positive comment on the organization or even something you see in the office.

- **Understand that a traditional interview is not a friendly exchange.** In a traditional interview situation, there is a job opening, and you will be one of several applicants for it. In this setting, the employer's task is to eliminate all applicants but one. The interviewer's questions are designed to elicit information that can be used to screen you out. And your objective is to avoid getting screened out. It's hardly an open and honest interaction, is it?

  Setting up interviews before an opening exists eliminates the stress of a traditional interview. In pre-interviews, employers are not trying to screen you out, and you are not trying to keep them from finding out stuff about you. Having said that, knowing how to answer questions that might be asked in a traditional interview is good preparation for any interview you face.

- **Be prepared to answer the tough interview questions.** Your answers to a few key problem questions may determine whether you get a job offer. There are simply too many possible interview questions to cover

(continued)

(continued)

one by one. Instead, 10 basic questions cover variations of most other interview questions. So, if you can learn to answer the Top 10 Problem Interview Questions well, you will know how to answer most others:

1. Why should I hire you?
2. Why don't you tell me about yourself?
3. What are your major strengths?
4. What are your major weaknesses?
5. What sort of pay do you expect to receive?
6. How does your previous experience relate to the jobs we have here?
7. What are your plans for the future?
8. What will your former employer (or references) say about you?
9. Why are you looking for this type of position, and why here?
10. Why don't you tell me about your personal situation?

- **Be prepared for the most important interview question of all.** "Why should I hire you?" is the most important question of all to answer well. Do you have a convincing argument why someone should hire you over someone else? If you don't, you probably won't get that job you really want. So think carefully about why someone should hire you and practice your response. Then make sure you communicate this in the interview, even if the interviewer never asks the question in a clear way.

Following Up with Thank-You Notes

It's a fact: People who follow up with potential employers and with others in their network get jobs more quickly than those who do not. Here are four rules to guide you in following up in your job search:

- Send a thank-you note or e-mail to every person who helps you in your job search.

- Send the note within 24 hours after speaking with the person.

- Enclose a JIST Card or e-mail signature with thank-you notes and all other correspondence.

- Develop a system to keep following up with good contacts.

There are several times in your job search when it's appropriate to send a thank-you note:

- **Before a job interview:** Offer sincere thanks for the chance to meet with the employer. Confirm the date and time of the interview and express your enthusiasm.

- **After a job interview:** This is one of the best times to send a thank-you note, and doing so over e-mail is acceptable. Remind the recipient why you are the best person for the job, clear up any weak areas in the interview, and show that you have good manners.

- **Whenever anyone helps you in your job search:** This includes those who give you referrals, people who provide advice, and simply those who are supportive during your search.

Following is an example of a simple thank-you note sent after an interview:

Dear Mr. O'Beel,

Thank you for the opportunity to interview for the position available in your production department. I want you to know that this is the sort of job I have been looking for and am enthusiastic about the possibility of working for you.

Now that we have spoken, I know that I have both the experience and skills to fit nicely into your organization and to be productive quickly. The process improvements I implemented at Logistics, Inc., increased the company's productivity 34 percent, and I am confident that I can do the same for you.

Thanks again for the interview. I enjoyed the visit.

Sincerely,

Sara Smith

(505) 665-0090

Appendix

ESSENTIAL JOB SEARCH DATA WORKSHEET

Take some time to complete this worksheet carefully. It will help you write your resume and answer interview questions. You can also photocopy it and take it with you to help complete applications and as a reference throughout your job search. Use an erasable pen or pencil to allow for corrections. Whenever possible, emphasize skills and accomplishments that support your ability to do the job you want. Use extra sheets as needed. You can also find this worksheet online at www.jist.com/pdf/EJSDW.pdf.

Your name _____

Date completed _____

Job objective _____

Key Accomplishments

List three accomplishments that best prove your ability to do the kind of job you want.

1. _____

2. _____

3. _____

Education and Training

Name of high school(s) and specific years attended _____

_____

Subjects related to job objective _____

_____

_____

Related extracurricular activities/hobbies/leisure activities _____

_____

_____

Accomplishments/things you did well _____

_____

_____

Specific things you can do as a result _____

_____

_____

**Schools you attended after high school, specific years attended, and
degrees/certificates earned** _____

_____

_____

Courses related to job objective _____

_____

_____

Related extracurricular activities/hobbies/leisure activities _____

_____

_____

Accomplishments/things you did well _____

_____

_____

Specific things you can do as a result _____

_____

_____

Other Training

Include formal or informal learning, workshops, military training, skills
you learned on the job or from hobbies—anything that will help support
your job objective. Include specific dates, certificates earned, or other
details as needed. _____

_____

_____

(continued)

(continued)

Work and Volunteer History

List your most recent job first, followed by each previous job. Military experience, unpaid or volunteer work, and work in a family business should be included here, too. If needed, use additional sheets to cover *all* significant paid or unpaid work experiences. Emphasize details that will help support your new job objective. Include numbers to support what you did: the number of people served over one or more years, number of transactions processed, percentage of sales increased, total inventory value you were responsible for, payroll of the staff you supervised, total budget responsible for, and so on. Emphasize results you achieved, using numbers to support them whenever possible. Mentioning these things on your resume and in an interview will help you get the job you want.

Job 1

Dates employed_____

Name of organization_____

Supervisor's name and job title_____

Address_____

_____

Phone number/e-mail address/Web site_____

_____

What did you accomplish and do well?_____

_____

Things you learned; skills you developed or used_____

_____

_____

Raises, promotions, positive evaluations, awards_____

_____

_____

Computer software, hardware, and other equipment you used_____

_____

_____

Other details that might support your job objective _____

_____

_____

Job 2

Dates employed _____

Name of organization _____

Supervisor's name and job title _____

Address _____

_____

Phone number/e-mail address/Web site ____ _____   _____

_____

What did you accomplish and do well? _____

_____

_____

Things you learned; skills you developed or used _____

_____

_____

Raises, promotions, positive evaluations, awards _____

_____

_____

Computer software, hardware, and other equipment you used _____

_____

_____

Other details that might support your job objective _____

_____

_____

(continued)

(continued)

Job 3

Dates employed_____

Name of organization_____

Supervisor's name and job title_____

Address_____

_____

Phone number/e-mail address/Web site_____

_____

What did you accomplish and do well?_____

_____

_____

Things you learned; skills you developed or used_____

_____

_____

Raises, promotions, positive evaluations, awards_____

_____

_____

Computer software, hardware, and other equipment you used_____

_____

_____

Other details that might support your job objective_____

_____

_____

References

Think of people who know your work well and will be positive about your work and character. Past supervisors are best. Contact them and tell them what type of job you want and your qualifications, and ask what they will say about you if contacted by a potential employer. Some employers will not provide references by phone, so ask them for a letter of reference in advance. If a past employer may say negative things, negotiate what they will say or get written references from others you worked with there.

Reference name _____

Position or title _____

Relationship to you _____

Contact information (complete address, phone number, e-mail address)

_____

_____

Reference name _____

Position or title _____

Relationship to you _____

Contact information (complete address, phone number, e-mail address)

_____

_____

Reference name _____

Position or title _____

Relationship to you _____

Contact information (complete address, phone number, e-mail address)

_____

_____